D1505348

THE GREAT EMPIRE OF CHINA

and Marco Polo in World History

Richard Worth

Enslow Publishers, Inc.

40 Industrial Road   PO Box 38
Box 398   Aldershot
Berkeley Heights, NJ 07922 Hants GU12 6BP
USA   UK

http://www.enslow.com

Library of Congress Cataloging-in-Publication Data

Worth, Richard.
    The great empire of China and Marco Polo in world history / Richard
Worth.
        p. cm. — (In world history)
        Includes bibliographical references and index.
        ISBN 0-7660-1939-X
        1. Polo, Marco, 1254-1323?—Juvenile literature. 2. Asia—Description
and travel—Early works to 1800—Juvenile literature. 3. Mongols—
History—Juvenile literature. I. Title. II. Series.
G370.P9 W67   2003
915.04'2'092—dc21
                                                            2002152264

Printed in the United States of America

10 9 8 7 6 5 4 3 2

To Our Readers: We have done our best to make sure all Internet Addresses in
this book were active and appropriate when we went to press. However, the
author and the publisher have no control over and assume no liability for the
material available on those Internet sites or on other Web sites they may link to.
Any comments or suggestions can be sent by e-mail to comments@enslow.com or
to the address on the back cover.

Illustration Credits: Charles Hogarth, *Illustrations of World-Famous
Places*, Dover Publications, Inc., New York, 1993, p. 18; Enslow
Publishers, Inc., pp. 6–7; Gustave Doré, *Doré's Illustrations of the
Crusades*, Dover Publications, Inc., New York, 1997, pp. 24, 26, 27; J. G.
Heck, *Heck's Pictorial Archive of Military Science, Geography, and History*,
Dover Publications, Inc., New York, 1994, pp. 32, 83, 88, 91; Reproduced
from the Collections of the Library of Congress, p. 10; *The Travels of
Marco Polo: The Complete Yule-Cordier Edition*, Dover Publications, Inc.,
volume 1, pp. 4, 14, 37, 40, 44, 46, 49, 58, 64, 67, 71, 95; *The Travels of
Marco Polo: The Complete Yule-Cordier Edition*, Dover Publications, Inc.,
volume 2, pp. 77, 78, 79, 100.

Cover Illustration: © Digital Vision Ltd. All rights reserved
(Background Map); *The Travels of Marco Polo: The Complete Yule-
Cordier Edition*, Dover Publications, Inc., volume 1 (Marco Polo
Portrait).

Contents

When Marco Polo, his uncle, and his father returned home from their journey, hardly anyone recognized them. They were even denied entrance into their home at first.

Chapter 1

Riches of the East

In 1295, three tired travelers returned home to Venice, Italy. They walked down the streets wearing tattered, old clothes. No one in Venice had seen clothes like these before—strange garments worn by the Mongols who had conquered much of Asia. The travelers looked like dirty beggars washed up on the shores of Venice. Two of the men were almost seventy, considered very old for that time when many Venetians did not live beyond thirty. The third traveler was much younger, just over forty.

The Polos

The three men were Marco Polo; his father, Niccolo; and his uncle, Maffeo. All of them were merchants. They had just completed a journey unlike any other undertaken by European travelers of that time. It had taken twenty-four years and covered almost fifteen thousand miles. The Polos had traveled from Venice, across Asia Minor (part of modern-day Turkey), to China (then called Cathay). There they spent almost twenty years in the court of the legendary Kublai Khan, the powerful Mongol emperor who ruled China. Khan had grown so fond of the Polos that he did not want them to leave. Indeed, Marco had become the great Khan's ambassador, traveling to Sri

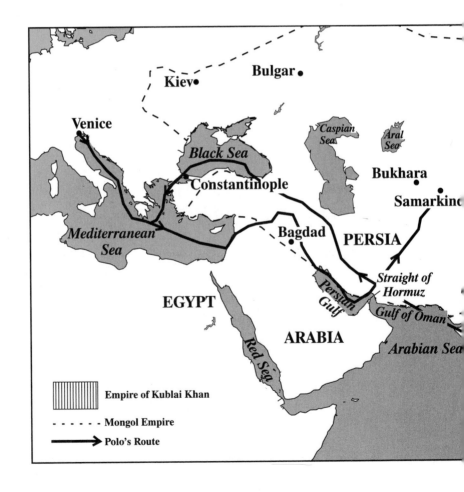

Lanka and India in southern Asia. Finally, in 1291, Kublai had asked the Polos to escort a beautiful seventeen-year-old princess, named Kokejin, to Persia (modern-day Iran) in the Middle East. She was to become the bride of the Khan's great nephew Arghun, the king of Persia.

Pirates and Treasures

Before the Polos departed, Khan lavished them with priceless jewels as well as two gold plaques. The Polos

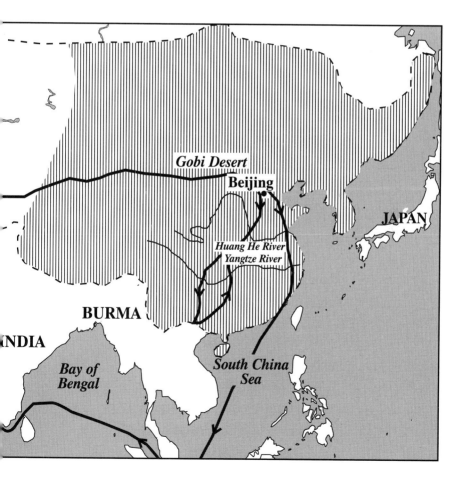

led a group of eighteen ships and an escort of almost six hundred soldiers from China down the coast of Asia to Sumatra, in present-day Indonesia. By the time they reached India, they were attacked by pirates who swarmed along the coast waiting for unsuspecting travelers. According to historian Richard Humble, "As soon as a likely victim was sighted the whole fleet would be alerted by means of beacon signals [from fires] passed down the line [of pirate ships], making it virtually impossible for a merchant ship to get through undetected."[1]

Surrounded by Death

By the time the Polos reached Persia, only eighteen people out of the original six hundred remained. It is not known why or how they died. The survivors arrived to find that Arghun had died. Nevertheless, Kokejin found a new husband, the king's son, Ghazan. From Persia, the Polos headed north to the Black Sea where they were forced to pay off the local ruler so they could pass through. "At last, by the grace of God, after much time and many labors," wrote Marco Polo, "we came to . . . Constantinople [in present-day Turkey]."[2] From here, the Polos finally returned to Venice.

Home in Venice

Venice is a city of canals, built along the waters of the Adriatic Sea. These canals serve as streets. The Polos probably traveled by gondola—a long, narrow, flat-bottomed boat—almost to the steps of their former home. Relatives were living there. The Polos looked far different from the merchants who had left Venice more than two decades earlier. At first, their relatives did not recognize them. In fact, the Polos had been gone for so long, most of the people had assumed they had been killed by the Mongols. The Mongols had a reputation as ruthless warriors.

Eventually the Polos convinced everyone that they were exactly who they said they were. They also insisted that they were anything but beggars, but wealthy merchants. No one, however, believed them.

According to one story, the Polos then arranged to hold a great banquet at their home and invited a large number of people. As the banquet began, the Polos were dressed in fancy clothes. Obviously, they had somehow acquired the money to buy these clothes in Venice. But the surprises had just begun. At one point during the banquet, the Polos left the room and returned wearing the original old clothes that they had worn on their arrival in Venice. Then they held up sharp knives, ripped open the clothes, and revealed precious stones hidden beneath. These included rubies and emeralds.[3] These were the riches that had been given to the Polos by Kublai Khan. They had managed to hide them during the journey home so they would not be stolen. Now, everyone seemed convinced that these were the Polos.

The Polos were given great honors by the city. Maffeo, for example, became a Venetian official. And many people came to talk with Marco. But they were still not entirely ready to believe the tales of his

Christopher Columbus (pictured) was influenced by Marco Polo's famous book A Description of the World.

adventures. No one they knew had ever been to China. Marco's descriptions of his travels and the court of Kublai Khan seemed much too extraordinary to be believed.

Recording the Adventure

Eventually, Marco Polo would publish a book of his adventures. Even then, people continued to doubt what he said and felt sure that his tales were exaggerated. Only after his death did Marco Polo's *A Description of The World* begin to influence mapmakers and explorers. It was printed and reprinted, and circulated throughout Europe. In fact, during the fifteenth century, Christopher Columbus read Marco Polo's descriptions and regarded them as a guide for his own explorations across the Atlantic Ocean in search of China and Japan.

Marco Polo's travels and his writings would eventually leave a profound mark on the history of the world.

Chapter 2

Citizens of Venice

The Polo family came to Venice in the eleventh century. They had originally lived in Dalmatia, an area along the eastern coast of the Adriatic Sea, located in present-day Croatia.

The Polos were merchants and traders. By 1250, there were three brothers who carried on the family trading business. Maffeo and Niccolo lived in Venice, not too far from St. Mark's Church, a prominent cathedral in the city. Here in Venice, Niccolo and his wife had a son named Marco Polo in 1254. The oldest Polo brother, also named Marco, may have lived in Constantinople. This city was located at the southern entrance to the Black Sea in Asia Minor. Since there was a brisk trade between Venice and Constantinople, the Polos probably maintained a representative there to protect their business interests. They also had a trading station farther north, near the Black Sea. This was another profitable area of trade, between Venice and the people who lived in Russia.

The Beginnings of Venice

By 1254, the Republic of Venice was the most successful trading nation in western Europe. (Today Venice is a city in the nation of Italy.) The rise of Venice was not an overnight success. A thousand years earlier, in fact, there was no Venice. Rome was the most important city in Italy. The Romans ruled a vast empire that stretched northward into Europe, eastward into Asia Minor, and south across the Mediterranean Sea into Egypt. Although Rome had a very powerful army, it was not strong enough to prevent increasing pressure from European tribes. The tribes wanted more and more land that was part of the Roman Empire. In the fifth century A.D., Attila led the Huns, a tribe from north-central Asia, into Italy. They destroyed many Roman cities and even threatened Rome itself. Seeking safety, many people in northern Italy fled their homes and resettled along the coast of the Adriatic Sea.

These refugees established small settlements in the marshes and lagoons that were formed by the salt waters of the Adriatic Sea. By A.D. 493, Italy fell to a tribe called the Ostrogoths and their powerful king, Theodoric. A century later, another tribe, the Lombards, invaded. Fearing that these tribes would threaten their settlements, many northern Italians living near the Adriatic moved even farther east to a series of islands on the coast. These islands provided more protection from the Lombards, who were not a seafaring people. Since Rome had fallen, the people along the Adriatic Sea became part of a vast territory ruled by Constantinople. Constantinople was the new capital of the Roman Empire. It had been established by the emperor Constantine in the fourth century A.D.

At first, the towns along the Adriatic remained fairly independent. During the ninth century, however, they were threatened by another invasion. This time the invaders came from an area in present-day Germany, led by Pepin of Herstal. He was the son of Charlemagne, king of the Franks, a Germanic tribe. Although Pepin succeeded in capturing several towns on the Adriatic, many people moved to an island named Rivo Alto. Here they defended themselves against Pepin and his army. Rivo Alto, later known simply as the Rialto, became the site on which Venice was founded. The island was marshy, with many channels cut by the waters of the Adriatic Sea. These channels were eventually dug into canals. These canals, used as roads, became the primary means of transportation in Venice. Homes were built along the canals. Gondolas took the Venetians from one part of their city to another. From wharves, or piers, larger ships could access the great trading routes of medieval Europe by way of the Adriatic Sea.

13

This picture of twentieth-century Venice shows one of the city's many canals. A gondola is docked near a building.

A City Built on Trade

During the Middle Ages (A.D. 400s–1500s), Venice began to build a large trading empire. Because of their location, Venetians possessed something that was essential to the lives of people throughout the medieval world: salt. The lagoons and marshes around Venice trapped salt water from the Adriatic Sea. The Venetians gathered the salt and sold it. Salt was valuable because it was used to preserve meat and fish. No refrigerators or freezers existed in this period. Unless meat or fish was eaten immediately after it was killed or caught, it would go bad. However, meat and fish could be packed in salt and preserved for long periods. As one historian explained: "Salt, therefore, was a precious commodity. And because of her position in the salt marshes, Venice had almost a monopoly [complete control] on salt."[1] To keep this monopoly, the Venetians also went to war with nearby towns to prevent them from using the salt in their areas. Venetian ships carried salt east to Constantinople. They also transported it west into the Mediterranean to French and Spanish cities.

In addition to salt, Venetian ships carried other goods. Near Venice were dense forests. The trees were cut for wood that the Venetians took to many cities to be used in building ships, constructing homes, and making furniture. In northern Italy were vast fields of wheat. Wheat was also carried in Venetian ships to many parts of the world. The wheat was used to make bread. Once the Venetian ships arrived in foreign ports, their merchants sold their goods. Then they picked up other goods that could be sold elsewhere or brought back to Venice. These included furs from the area around the Black Sea, cotton from Egypt, and gold from Africa.

The Trip East

While some Venetian traders ventured only along the shores of Europe and Africa, others traveled overland to the Far East. They braved the dangers of robbers to travel across the mountains and deserts of central Asia to China, India, and Southeast Asia. From these places, merchants like the Polos carried back spices, silk, and diamonds and other precious stones. There was also another valuable cargo transported by the Polos and other Venetian traders: slaves.

Slavery

Slavery had existed since the time of the Sumerians, who lived in much of present-day Iraq from 3500 B.C. to 2000 B.C. Slaves were often prisoners of war. They were forced to work without pay. The ancient Assyrians, Babylonians, Egyptians, Persians, Greeks, and Romans all had slaves. During the Middle Ages, many of the slaves were Slavonic people from Russia and Hungary. The slaves were sold to Venetian merchants who carried them to other parts of Europe. Slaves were sold in the marketplaces of Egypt and other cities of the Middle East. They were also sold to families in Italy, and transported to cities along the coast and on islands in the Mediterranean Sea. There they toiled on sugar plantations.

Convoys and Galleys

The Venetian merchants, like the Polos, were courageous sailors. They braved the treacherous seas of the Mediterranean and the Adriatic in small ships. These ships included merchant vessels with a triangular, or lateen, sail as well as galleys. The galleys carried not only a sail, but also banks of oarsmen to propel the ship when there was little or no wind. As historian Henry Hart wrote:

> The crews were freemen, so many of them Slavonians from the Dalmatian coast. . . . No seaman could be under eighteen years of age . . . and each was under oath to obey the laws of Venice. Crews were hired for the shipping season—from March 1 through November 30—and were paid in advance every three months. . . . The ship was fitted out with trumpets, drums, and kettledrums, used for routine calls to duty, to mark the time, and, in case of a fight, to arouse and sustain the courage of the crew.[2]

The Venetian ships generally traveled in a large group, called a convoy. This was a way to protect themselves from deadly pirates who stalked the coastlines. The convoys would leave from Venice to go to many places, including Alexandria, Egypt; Constantinople; Syria in the Middle East; the Black Sea; as well as England and the Netherlands.

A ship might be owned by a single trading business like the one run by the Polos. But most often, Venetians would invest in a merchant trading company. The trading company would finance a fleet of ships that sailed along one of the trade routes. Merchants and investors would often meet along the Rialto to make their arrangements.

After the convoys had sailed, they would await word of the ships along the Rialto—the center of Venice. In the play *Merchant of Venice*, William Shakespeare included the words: "What news on the Rialto?" This referred to the well-known Venetian

The Rialto Bridge spans the Grand Canal in Venice. It was first built in the eleventh century as a wooden bridge, but has since been redesigned and reconstructed many times.

habit of waiting along the Rialto for news of one's investment in a trading venture.

If such a venture were successful, the investors could make a large amount of money on cargoes of gold, precious jewels, and slaves. These were sold for large profits. However, a convoy could also meet with disaster at the hands of ruthless pirates or stormy seas. Trading was a risk. Only adventurers, like the Polos, were prepared to risk their fortunes and their lives each time they set out on a new journey.

The Mighty Rulers of Venice

Venice was an *oligarchy*. In this type of government, power is controlled by the few. At the head of the Venetian government was the duke of Venice, known as the *doge*. The first doge was selected by the people of Venice, including the aristocrats, priests, and craftsmen, at the end of the seventh century.

At first, the position of doge was very powerful. The doge was considered a king, and dressed himself in rich clothes. He selected every court official and commanded the Venetian navy that protected the merchant ships from harm. Although the doge was elected, the position of doge was controlled by only a few wealthy families for several centuries. As historian Thomas Chubb wrote: ". . . most doges saw to it that their successors were named while they were still living— usually a son or at least a relative."[3]

Gradually, the doge's position became so powerful that the wealthy merchants decided that their authority had to be curbed. During the eleventh century, the merchants appointed councilors to act as a check on the power of the doge. They also succeeded in preventing the doge from exercising so much control over naming his successor. By the twelfth century, the number of councilors had increased to as many as sixteen hundred people. They came primarily from upper class families, and along with the doge, they ran Venice. Small committees of the Great Council, as it was called, carried on the day-to-day governing of Venice. Together, these people comprised the oligarchy that controlled the city. Many of the merchant fleets were paid for by Venice itself. Large profits helped turn Venice into one of the most magnificent cities in Europe.

During the late Middle Ages, one visitor wrote: "Venice is the most triumphant city I have ever seen. It is the one that does the greatest honor to ambassadors and foreigners. . . . It may have faults. It does. But I firmly believe that the Almighty forever guides its destinies." Another visitor wrote, "I never look out my window, that I do not see a thousand merchants in as many gondolas." And the well-to-do, he added, "gleam in silk and gold and jewels."[4]

A Great Nation of Merchants

By the time of the Polos, Venice had become a successful trading empire. This was mainly due to the skill of its merchants and the power of its navy. This did not happen overnight, however. Venice had achieved its position as a result of many hard-won victories. Some of these had been at the expense of the pirates along the Dalmatian coast. For a time, they had been paid to stay away from the Venetian merchant ships. But these bribes did not guarantee safety. The merchants were still attacked by the Dalmatian pirates.

Finally, at the beginning of the eleventh century, a doge named Pietro Orseolo II led the Venetian fleet against the pirates. He won a series of victories that greatly reduced their power. The Venetians took control of cities along the Dalmatian coast. Then they defeated other pirate ships from present-day Hungary and Croatia. Venetian control was also extended into parts of present-day Greece and Albania.

During the latter part of the eleventh century, the Venetians faced another menace. An army from Normandy in France had invaded southern Italy and taken control of many Italian cities. This new threat could easily disrupt the Venetian trading routes. In addition, the Normans were threatening the territories controlled by the Byzantine Empire from its capital in Constantinople.

Byzantine emperor Alexius Comnenus and the Venetian doge Domenico Selvo decided that the Normans must be stopped. First, the Venetians were successful in defeating a Norman fleet. But the Normans, unwilling to give in, continued the war and sent out another fleet. This fleet, too, was defeated by the Venetians.

Alexius Comnenus was very grateful to the Venetians for their triumph over the Normans. He gave Venice trading stations in Constantinople along the water. He also added "full exemption from all taxes and customs duties for Venetian merchants throughout the Empire."

"The importance of this last concession," wrote historian John Julius Norwich, "is almost impossible to exaggerate. Suddenly, the Venetians found immense territories which, for all practical purposes, they could consider as their own."[5] The Venetians had become the premier merchants for the entire empire.

Constantinople

The Byzantine Empire stretched across Asia Minor and the Middle East. Located on a narrow strait that separates the Aegean Sea from the Black Sea, Constantinople was ideally situated to control important trading routes during the Middle Ages.

Source Document

The circumference of the city of Constantinople is eighteen miles. . . . At Constantinople is the place of worship called St. Sophia. . . . It is ornamented with pillars of gold and silver, and with innumerable lamps of the same precious metals. . . . King Manuel has built a large palace for his residence on the seashore. . . . The pillars and walls are covered with pure gold, and all the wars of the ancients, as well as his own wars, are represented in pictures. The throne in this palace is of gold, and ornamented with precious stones. The Greeks . . . dress in garments of silk, ornamented with gold and other valuable materials.[6]

Above, a twelfth-century traveler to Constantinople describes the grand city.

Holy Wars

Although the empire was large and wealthy, the Byzantine emperors did not have an easy time defending it. They were constantly threatened by powerful enemies such as the Normans and the Muslims. The Muslims were the followers of Islam. This new religion had been founded by the prophet Mohammed in the early seventh century. After Mohammed's death in A.D. 632, the Muslims began to extend their religion to other parts of the world. They conquered most of North Africa and the Middle East, including the city of Jerusalem. According to the Muslim tradition, Mohammed ascended from Jerusalem into heaven. Jerusalem is sacred to the Muslims.

During the eleventh and twelfth centuries, the popes in Rome called on the Christians throughout Europe to throw the Muslims out of the city of Jerusalem. This city was considered sacred throughout Christendom. It had been the site of the crucifixion of Jesus Christ. It was also the city from which he had, according to Christian teachings, ascended into heaven. In 1095, Pope Urban II called a crusade that succeeded in retaking Jerusalem from the Muslims. The Venetians, who owned a large fleet, transported the crusaders on their victorious campaign to the Middle East. Once the crusaders had established themselves there, the Venetian fleet also helped them conquer other Muslim cities along the coast.

While the Venetians were extending their power in the Middle East, their position in the Byzantine

The First Crusade was a series of bloody battles that took place from 1096 to 1099. Here, Christian Crusaders (top left) fight Muslim Turks (bottom right).

Empire was weakening. The Byzantine emperors had grown tired of allowing the Venetians to enjoy enormous trading advantages. That which benefited the Venetians reduced the amount of money being collected in taxes by the Byzantine state. During the latter part of the twelfth century, the Byzantine rulers withdrew these privileges. The emperors took possession of the Venetian ships in Constantinople and murdered all the Venetian traders there.

But the Venetians would soon be given a chance to take revenge. In 1187, the Christians lost control of Jerusalem to the Muslim leader Saladin. A crusade was launched, led by Richard the Lion Hearted, King of England, to retake Jerusalem. But it was unsuccessful in winning back the city. The crusaders launched another effort against the Muslims in 1201. They made an arrangement with the Venetians to carry a new army to Jerusalem to retake the city. The Venetians, led by their doge, Enrico Dandolo, had bargained hard and received a huge sum of money to carry the Christian army. However, the Christians were unable to raise the agreed-upon sum. Dandolo told them that, in return for not paying the full amount, they must join him in putting down a revolt in the city of Zara in Dalmatia. This city had been controlled by the Venetians before Zara had become independent.

Dandolo, doge of Venice (center with hands raised), promises the Crusaders ships and supplies in exchange for a small payment and half of all conquered territories in the east.

The Conquest of Constantinople

Once the expedition against Zara was successful, the Venetians decided that they would sail on to Constantinople. A Byzantine emperor, who had been forced off his throne by rebels, asked for the help of the crusaders and the Venetians. He wanted them to

The fall of Constantinople was a black mark in the history of Venice. Venetians and other Crusaders massacred citizens of the city, causing the Greeks to retreat.

restore him to the throne. In 1203, the allies attacked Constantinople. Dandolo, who was blind and already in his eighties, led the Venetian Navy. According to one observer, he "stood fully armed on the prow [front part] of his galley . . . and cried out to his men to drive the ship ashore if they valued their skins. And so they did, and ran the galley ashore, and he and they leapt down and planted the banner before him in the ground."[7]

Constantinople fell to the allies. They then demanded their payment from the new emperor. He had promised to give them a lot of money for helping him. But he could not afford to pay them. In April 1204, they turned on him and attacked the city. The attack was over quickly and the new emperor fled the capital. The crusaders and the Venetians then looted homes, government buildings, and churches, murdering many of the citizens of Constantinople.

For the Venetians, however, the attack was an enormous triumph. The Venetian rights throughout the Byzantine Empire were fully restored. The Venetians also took over ports on the Black Sea, Greece, and other areas. As a result, Venice was the leading trading nation throughout the entire area.

Chapter 3

The Polos and the Mongol Empire

In 1253, Niccolo and Maffeo Polo set sail from Venice on a trading voyage that would take them to Constantinople. Their ship headed south through the Adriatic Sea, around the Greek islands and northward through the Hellespont. This was the narrow waterway that separated Asia Minor from Europe. Finally, after several weeks on rough seas, the Polos arrived at Constantinople.

The Polos in Constantinople

By 1253, Constantinople had not fully recovered from the destruction caused by the crusaders and Venetians almost a half century earlier. "Innumerable structures, both public and private, had never been rebuilt in the interval since 1204," wrote historian Henry Hart,

Many that were still standing had been stripped of their copper roofs, bronze ornaments, lead, and tiles. Ruined walls and churches, palaces, and dwellings were on every side. The imperial palaces themselves had been so befouled and neglected that they were no longer fit for human occupation. . . . Such parts of the city as had been spared or rebuilt were crowded together, hovels and tenements shoulder to shoulder with palaces, churches and markets.[1]

Nevertheless, the Venetians still maintained a powerful political position in Constantinople. They were among an estimated sixty thousand western traders who were working in the city. Over the next six years, the Polos remained in Constantinople. The Polo brothers traded in furs, jewels, and probably slaves.[2] They received top prices for their goods and increased their wealth.

By the end of the decade, however, the political situation in Constantinople was changing. Michael Paleologus, an heir to the Byzantine emperor who had been ousted in 1204, had enlisted the aid of Genoa to regain the throne. The traders of Genoa, located in Italy, were rivals of the Venetians. It appeared as if Paleologus and the Genoese might be successful. This would mean that the Venetians would lose their trading position in Constantinople. The Polos decided that it was no longer safe for them to remain in the city. So, they gathered up all their goods and left. They relocated their business at Soldaia on the northern coast of the Black Sea. Since they already maintained a trading post in this town, it was easy for them to move their headquarters there.

From Soldaia, the Polos began traveling eastward. They traded with Germanic peoples, Tartars, and Greeks who inhabited Asia Minor. Eventually, they reached the lands of the powerful Mongol Empire. In 1261, the Polos entered one of the principal Mongol cities, Bolgara, located on the Volga River in Russia.

The Wandering Mongols

The Mongols came from the high region, called a plateau, of Mongolia in eastern Asia. They were nomads, or wanderers, who moved from place to place. They tended large flocks of sheep and herds of cattle. These animals provided all the necessary elements of life for the Mongols. The sheep and cattle provided meat for the Mongols and their families. The sheep's wool was used for clothing. The Mongols also made woolen felt from the coats of the sheep to build their tents. These huge tents, called yurts, were created by stretching large pieces of felt over long wooden poles. They could be taken down easily so the Mongols could move them to new campgrounds. The Mongols spent summers in the northern plateau. As winter approached, the nomadic families moved south with their herds to warmer climates.

The Rise of the Mongols

The Mongols were formidable soldiers. Mongol clans or tribes formed small contingents of cavalry, or soldiers on horses. What made these cavalrymen so dangerous was their unrivaled ability as archers. From childhood, the Mongols developed their skill with bow and arrow. They could successfully shoot from horseback because their feet were fitted into stirrups that hung from the horse's sides. Therefore, they could stay in the saddle without holding on with their hands. This left them free to shoot.

The stirrup may have originated as early as the second century B.C. in China. It was also used by the Huns, who invaded Rome during the sixth century A.D. With the stirrup and their capability as archers, the Mongols gradually created a powerful force of cavalry. One of the leaders of these cavalry troops was Yesugei Bat'atur. Along the Mongolian plateau, Yesugei and his horsemen were engaged in constant conflict with

Here, Tartars are seen on horseback.

their arch rivals, the Tartars. The Tartars eventually poisoned Yesugei around 1176. He left behind a wife and a nine-year-old son, named Temujin.

Genghis Khan

After Yesugei's death, his powerful rivals within the Mongol tribe kidnapped Temujin. Eventually, Temujin succeeded in escaping from his kidnappers while they were engaged in a celebration. As Temujin grew, he developed his skills as a warrior. Gradually, he began to attract many warriors to him. Soon he began to lead them in campaigns against other tribes on the plateau. Temujin won many battles. His influence began to grow until he took control of a large territory on the eastern part of the high plateau. By 1204, he had successfully conquered all the other tribes in the area. Before Temujin, the Mongols were just many separate clans. If it were not for his efforts, the clans would not have become a strong, unified military force. Two years later, the Mongols proclaimed Temujin, Genghis Khan (Universal Ruler).

Over the next few years, Genghis Khan strengthened his hold on the Mongolian plateau and improved his army. He created a personal bodyguard of ten thousand outstanding troops. These men were loyal only to Genghis Khan. He also created new army units that were not based on single Mongolian clans, or tribes. The men were moved out of their clans and mixed with men from other clans to form new units. In this way, the soldiers were not tied to their clans but to the Mongolian Army and, ultimately, to Genghis Khan himself.

Genghis Khan ordered all Mongol males to be drafted into the army once they reached the age of fourteen. Then they might be assigned to the heavy cavalry or the light cavalry. Author Robert Marshall points out that:

> . . . if he was part of the heavy cavalry [a soldier] was given a coat of mail [metal links] and a cuirass [light armor] made of leather-covered iron scales. Each soldier carried a leather-covered wicker shield and a helmet of either leather or iron, depending on his rank. He was armed with two . . . bows and a large quiver containing no fewer than sixty arrows. Light cavalry carried a small sword and two or three javelins, while the heavy brigade carried a scimitar [sword], a battle axe or a mace and a 12-foot lance.[3]

Genghis Khan and his military commanders trained their soldiers relentlessly. One of the favorite tactics of Mongol horsemen was to pretend to retreat in the face of the enemy. The enemy cavalry would follow a small body of Mongols until they had been drawn into a trap created by the main Mongol army. Then the army would charge from all sides and defeat their foes. Since most of the Mongol soldiers could not read, their leaders set up a system of flags and signals. These were used to direct various groups of cavalry in battle. In addition, Genghis Khan maintained communications between the different parts of his Mongolian Empire with teams of riders. They would quickly carry messages from one place to another, often covering many miles in a single day.

The Empire Expands

By 1210, Genghis Khan had created a powerful army of Mongolian cavalry. But the army could not simply remain inactive. It cost far too much to maintain it. Genghis Khan had to look for wealthy empires to invade on his borders. If he could capture their towns and steal their riches, then he could enrich his horsemen. South of the Mongolian plateau lay the wealthy lands of northern China. These were controlled by the Chin Empire. The empire in northern China was created by conquerors called the Manchus, who named their empire after an earlier Chinese dynasty.

Over the next three years, Genghis Khan led successive invasions of the Chin lands. The Mongolian horsemen wreaked havoc among the Chinese towns and villages. They looted, burned, and killed, enriching themselves along the way. However, they were powerless to take control of the major Chin cities, which were protected by thick walls. The Mongols had not yet mastered the art of siege warfare. To capture a walled town using siege warfare, soldiers needed heavy weapons. These included catapults. The catapults were huge weapons that hurled heavy rocks against the walls. The rocks created holes so the invading army could attack through them and capture a city. Also during siege warfare, attackers would not allow any food, water, or enemy soldiers into the defending city. This would greatly weaken soldiers inside, so that they would be unfit to fight once the city walls were broken apart.

In 1214, the Mongols returned to China. This time they had learned enough from the Chinese to lay siege to the Chin capital at Chung-tu (present-day Beijing). After a long siege, the city finally fell to the Mongols. The Mongols destroyed the entire city. They massacred tens of thousands of Chinese. Inflicting a bloody punishment on the cities they conquered was a tactic that the Mongols would use over and over again. It was a way of sending a message to others who might oppose them. This was designed to convince other cities to give up without a fight. Many decided to surrender without putting up a battle.

Genghis Khan Turns West

Genghis Khan believed that his army was now strong enough to invade the rich empires of the West. One of these empires, the northern Persian Empire, stretched from Persia into southern Russia. It was ruled by the Khwarazm Shah. The capital of this great empire was the city of Samarkand. As historian Robert Marshall wrote:

> By some accounts, it was a magnificent city of some 500,000 inhabitants, a community of craftsmen, merchants, Chinese artisans, leather workers, goldsmiths and silversmiths. . . . The streets were lined with shady trees, cooled by fountains and decorated with gardens, and under Khwarazm Shah [it] became one of the most magnificent cities in Asia.[4]

During the thirteenth century, Samarkand was one of the most impressive cities in Asia.

From 1216 to 1218, Genghis Khan tried to establish trading relations with this empire. Each time, he was rebuffed by Khwarazm Shah. In 1218, a group of 450 Mongol merchants was murdered by the Persians.

In 1219, with an army that may have been as large as two hundred thousand men, Genghis Khan invaded the Khwarazm Shah's empire. A year later, Bukhara in the Shah's empire fell to the Mongol army. They destroyed the entire city. The inhabitants of Samarkand were so frightened that they surrendered without much of a fight. Many of the men were slaughtered. The women and children were sold into slavery.

The Mongols had taken over the entire empire. Meanwhile, Khwarazm Shah had fled his capital, and he died two years later.

While Genghis Khan had been subduing the empire in the west, the Chin empire overcame the soldiers he had left in northern China. They took back control of much of the territory that they had lost. Before Genghis Khan could lead an army against them, he died in 1227, at about the age of sixty.

The Mongols Reach Europe

After his death, the lands that Genghis Khan had conquered were divided among his sons. They had helped lead his armies to victory in China and the West. Among these sons was Batu, who ruled the lands around the Caspian Sea, called the Golden Horde. Another son, Ogodei, took his father's place as Great Khan. In 1230, Ogodei ordered a renewed invasion of China. By 1234, the Chin empire was completely destroyed. The Mongols took complete control of the area. Meanwhile Ogodei had also begun to build a great capital at Qaraqorum on the Mongolian plateau.

While the Mongols were conquering northern China, they had not forgotten about other lands that lay to the west. In 1236, Batu directed a campaign against the Bulgars. It resulted in the fall of their capital city of Bolgara on the Volga River. By this time, the Mongols had fully mastered the art of siege warfare. They carried catapults and other devices necessary for a long siege. In 1240, the Mongols advanced across the heart of Russia. They laid siege to Kiev on the Dnieper River, captured it, and destroyed the city.

In 1241, the Mongols marched into present-day Hungary and Poland. On April 9, 1241, they met an army of European knights at Liegnitz in western Poland. The heavily armored knights were lured into a trap by the Mongols. The mounted bowmen then surrounded the slower-moving knights. They were massacred by the thousands. Meanwhile another army of knights was defeated in Hungary. The Mongols seemed poised for an invasion of western Europe. But in 1242, the Great Khan, Ogodei, died. This set off a struggle for power in the Mongol Empire. Western Europe was saved from invasion as the Mongols retreated.

The Mongol Empire Encountered by the Polos

The Mongol Empire entered a period of instability. First one leader named Guyuk became Great Khan, only to die after a few years. He was followed by Mongke, who became Great Khan in 1248. Under his leadership the empire continued to expand. Mongol troops led by the Great Khan's brother, Hülegü, continued to push westward. In 1258, Hülegü sacked the Muslim city of Baghdad in present-day Iraq. The Mongols swept into Syria with an army estimated at three hundred thousand men. They brought their catapults and other siege engines to the walls of Aleppo, which fell in 1260. In the east, Mongke and his brother Kublai led a huge army to victory over the Chinese.

Mongke died in 1261, which temporarily stopped the advance of the Mongols. By then, they ruled the largest empire that the world had ever seen. About this time, Niccolo and Maffeo Polo entered the empire. They traveled to the Mongol city of Bolgara on the Volga River. The city was ruled by Barka Khan, the brother of Batu, who had died earlier. Barka welcomed the Polos, who gave him a generous gift of expensive jewels.

The Polos had hoped to remain in Bolgara for only a year and then return to Venice. But a civil war had broken out between Barka and Hülegü. Travel westward was barred by Hülegü's soldiers. So the Polos decided to head east toward Bokhara. This was a large

The city of Bolgara was eventually abandoned by its inhabitants and was in ruins by the early fifteenth century.

trading center. It lay astride one of the trade routes that connected China with the West. The Polos set off in large wagons for a trip that took them over treacherous rivers and through dry desert land. Reaching Bokhara, they saw a beautiful city. As historian Henry Hart wrote:

> It was surrounded by ramparts [protective walls], above which rose the blue domes and tiled walls of mosques [Muslim places of worship], gleaming in the sunshine. . . . Its shops were overflowing with the merchandise of the East—silks, porcelain, ivory, spices, and cunningly wrought metal work.[5]

The Rise of Kublai Khan

The Polos remained in Bokhara for three years. Civil strife made it impossible for them to travel either east or west. In 1265, the people of Bokhara received visitors from the court of Kublai Khan. Kublai had been born in China in 1215. He was a grandson of Genghis Khan. Most of his early life was spent in northern China, not in the Mongol capital of Qaraqorum. As a result, Kublai absorbed the customs of the Chinese. Along with his brother Mongke, he had led a successful campaign against the Chin dynasty.

Following the death of Mongke in 1260, Kublai Khan announced that he would succeed to the throne as the Great Khan. However, he was opposed by some leaders who suspected that he was more Chinese than Mongol. Indeed, Khan had built a new capital for himself in China, called Chengdu. Eventually, Kublai

Khan overcame his rivals. From the city of Chengdu, he ruled the Mongol Empire.

The Polos Travel to China

When Kublai Khan's messengers reached Bokhara, they visited with the Polos. They told the two brothers that their emperor wanted to see them and learn more about the people of the West. Niccolo and Maffeo grabbed this opportunity to leave Bokhara. For the next year, they made the journey eastward with Kublai Khan's men. The journey took them across the mountains and deserts of central Asia. Finally they reached the palace of Kublai Khan.

Here the Polos met the emperor. The Great Khan warmly welcomed the two traders. He told them of his deep interest in learning more about Christianity as it was practiced in the West. He even wanted them to return and talk to the pope in Rome about sending teachers to convert the Mongols to the Christian religion. Christianity was not unknown in the Mongol Empire. Indeed, the Mongols tolerated all religious beliefs. They only required that conquered peoples bow down before the emperor and pay their taxes.

Christians from the Middle East had already spread their ideas throughout large parts of the Mongol Empire. These Christians were called Nestorians. They were followers of Nestorius, a religious leader in Constantinople during the fifth century. Communities of Nestorians had sprung up in cities such as Samarkand and Bokhara. When these cities were conquered by the Mongols, Nestorian Christianity began to spread throughout the empire. Its religious beliefs were somewhat different from those of the Catholic Church in Rome. For example, Catholics believe in a Holy Trinity, consisting of God the Father; Jesus Christ, the Son; and the Holy Ghost. Nestorians believed in only two persons in one God, the Father and the Son.

In addition to the influence of Nestorians, the pope in Rome had also sent envoys to the Mongols. They had traveled into the empire during the 1240s. These messengers included monks who belonged to the order of Dominicans and the order of Franciscans. The Dominican order was founded by St. Dominic in 1216. The Dominicans were committed to lives of poverty and preaching. The Franciscans were founded about the same time by St. Francis of Assisi. They were also committed to teaching and helping the poor.

The Golden Plaque

Kublai Khan gave the Polo brothers a golden plaque. This was a symbol of the great emperor's protection. Then he sent them on their way westward to Europe. They carried a letter from him asking the pope to send a group of learned priests who could tell him more about Christianity. He also indicated that the Mongols might convert to Christianity if he was convinced that it was the only true religion. Whether Khan was serious or not is uncertain. He may have simply wanted the expertise of learned men from the West to help him with his empire. It was an enormous empire to govern.[6]

Having received imperial protection, the Polos headed west in 1266. It was a long journey, lasting three years. They retraced their steps through Bokhara, then journeyed into Persia and Syria. Eventually, they reached the city of Acre on the coast of the Mediterranean Sea. There they met with an ambassador of the pope, named Theobald. He told them that Pope Clement IV had died. Therefore, they must wait for a new pope to be selected before they could deliver their message from Kublai Khan. As a result, the Polos decided to sail for Venice. They arrived home in 1269.

In this illustration from the fourteenth century, the Polo brothers receive a gold plaque from the Great Khan.

The Polos had taken a tremendous journey into the heart of the Mongol Empire. Unlike most other Venetian traders, they had learned the Mongol language. They had also met the great leader of the vast Mongol Empire. And they had received his imperial protection while traveling throughout his lands, provided that they carried out their promise to come back. The stage had now been set for a return visit to bring back the Catholic priests. On this visit, they would take Niccolo's son, Marco Polo.

Marco Polo

Chapter 4

Marco Polo Travels to China

At the time of Marco Polo's birth in 1254, his father and uncle had already left for Constantinople. When he was still a boy, Marco's mother died. He was probably raised by relatives. Little is known of Marco's childhood. Historians guess that Marco and his cousins may have walked along the muddy roads to the most important sections of Venice. Indeed, they may have even gone to the piers to see some of the Venetian galleys leave on their voyages or return filled with goods.[1]

Young Marco Polo Goes to China

When Marco's father and uncle returned from China, Marco was already a young man of fifteen. They no doubt told him about their adventures. And, when Niccolo and Maffeo said they planned to return to

China, Marco was told that he could go with them. While Niccolo was in Venice, he married again, giving Marco a new stepmother. But the Polos had no intention of remaining in Venice for too long. Niccolo and Maffeo had promised Kublai Khan that they would return as soon as possible. They planned to bring learned priests from the Catholic Church as soon as the pope had selected them.

Unfortunately, the Catholic Curia, or council of cardinals, could not agree on a new pope. They traditionally elected a pope from among the cardinals. The Polos finally became too impatient to wait any longer. In 1271, they decided to begin their return journey to China. After leaving Venice, they traveled to Acre on the Mediterranean coast. Here they met with Theobald once again. The renowned religious leader gave them permission to obtain some sacred oil from the site of Jesus Christ's tomb in Jerusalem.

Kublai Khan had asked specifically for this oil when the Polos were last in China. Having also received a letter to the great Khan from Theobald, the Polos were ready to begin their journey east. A short distance from Acre, they received word that Theobald himself had been selected the new pope. He took the name of Gregory X. The Polos returned to Acre. Pope Gregory assigned two learned monks to accompany the Polos to China. They were the only men he could gather to bring the teachings of the Catholic Church to China. The two monks were Friar William of Tripoli, in North Africa, and Friar Nicholas of Vicenza, in

Italy. The monks carried letters from the pope. They also had the authority to create priests and bishops in China. The new priests and bishops would help spread Christianity among the people who lived in the empire of the Great Khan.

With these additions to their party, the Venetian travelers set out once again for China.

On the Road Through Persia

From Acre, the Polos had planned to head south through Syria and Iraq. However, they found that warfare blocked their route through Syria. A bloody conflict had broken out between the Mongols and the Mamelukes. The Mamelukes were a group of warriors who had taken control of Egypt during the thirteenth century. Under a powerful leader named Baybars, the Mamelukes extended their power into Syria. Here they proved to be better soldiers than the Mongols, pushing them back across Syria in a series of successful raids. The war frightened the two monks who were accompanying the Polos. As a result, the friars decided to leave the expedition and return to Acre.

The Polos, however, decided to make a wide arc that took them eastward through Armenia. Then they headed south through Persia. The route took them through Georgia, which borders the Caspian Sea. Here Marco encountered oil for the first time. Today, Georgia still has rich oil fields, and this "black gold," as it is called, is used to power industrial machines. During the Middle Ages, however, the modern value of this oil had not yet been realized. As Marco wrote:

> . . . there is a fountain from which oil springs in great abundance. . . . This oil is not good to use with food, but 'tis good to burn [in lamps], and is also used to anoint camels that have the mange [a skin disease]. People come from vast distances to fetch it, for in all the countries round about they have no other oil.[2]

From Georgia, the Polos traveled south to the town of Tabriz in Persia. As one historian wrote: "The travelers would have lodged in the Christian quarter, a neighborhood still known as the Qaleh, or fortress, because . . . it was separated from the Muslim community by a wall."[3] Among the Christians there were Nestorians.

Marco was also interested in the products that were made by the people in Persia and elsewhere as he passed through their towns. After all, he was a member of a trading family. So it was natural for him to be interested in all the products that towns might produce for sale. These goods included cloth made of silk, as well as buckram—a heavy form of cotton.

In the town of Saveh, farther south, Marco said he saw the graves of the three wise men. These noblemen had visited the infant Jesus in Bethlehem many centuries earlier. They had brought gifts of gold, frankincense, and myrrh. (Frankincense and myrrh are used to make incense and perfume.) Marco wrote that "they are buried, in three very large and beautiful monuments, side by side. And above them there is a square building, carefully kept. The bodies are still entire."[4] While Marco may have been told that the three wise men were there, no evidence supports this.

Bandits and Hot Winds

The Polos continued their journey south from Tabriz. Historians estimate that they traveled at the rate of about twenty-five miles a day on horses or donkeys. As they journeyed, the heat increased. Again the Polos had to travel through parched desert areas. Eventually, they reached Yazd. As historian Mike Edwards wrote: "It was an oasis, thanks to qanats, tunnels that brought water from mountains miles away."[5] Water made Yazd livable, and the local merchants carried on a brisk trade in silk garments that were manufactured there.

Marco discovered that the people mined turquoise in a nearby kingdom called Kerman. This was considered a precious stone used for jewelry in the medieval world. It created an important source of wealth for Kerman.

As the Polos continued their journey, they were attacked by bandits. At one point, they had to ride their horses furiously into a nearby town. The town was defended by thick walls, so the Polos were safe. After the highwaymen had disappeared, they continued traveling south to the town of Hormuz. This was a major port. Marco explained that merchants from India came to Hormuz carrying spices, pearls, and fine cloth to trade.

The weather in Hormuz became extremely hot during the summer. In fact, the residents of the city often left to find relief in the countryside. The nights

Source Document

[They] are very skillful in making [the] harness of war; their saddles, bridles, spurs, swords, bows, quivers, and arms of every kind, are very well made indeed according to the fashion of those parts. The ladies of the country and their daughters also produce exquisite needlework in the embroidery of silk stuffs in different colors, with figures of beasts and birds, trees and flowers, and a variety of other patterns.[6]

Marco Polo describes the people of Kerman.

became so hot that people often slept outside in their gardens. Hot winds blew across the countryside, intensifying the heat. To escape these terrible winds, people jumped into nearby streams and remained below the water, except for their heads, until the winds had passed.

Changing Direction

Marco's father and uncle considered taking a sea route from Hormuz to India and then north by land to China. But as they examined the ships that would take them to India, the Polos began to have second thoughts. "Their ships are wretched affairs, and many of them get lost; for they have no iron fastenings, and are only stitched together with twine made from the husk of the Indian nut," wrote Marco. He continued:

> [The ships] have one mast, one sail, and one rudder, and have no deck, but only a cover spread over the cargo when loaded. . . . Hence 'tis a perilous business to go a voyage in one of those ships, and many of them are lost, for in that Sea of India the storms are often terrible.[7]

So the Polos decided to head north, back to Kerman, then across a broad desert area into Afghanistan. By this time, it was probably 1273.

Across a Desert

As they crossed the desert, the Polos carried a supply of water with them. The water in the desert could not be drunk without causing severe diarrhea. Fortunately, the Polos finally reached a clear freshwater spring, where they could drink their fill. The Polos then traveled to the city of Kuh-banan. Here they could take on more food. They crossed another desert area and eventually came to a broad plain. Historian Richard Humble wrote:

> Here stood one of the oddest natural landmarks . . . the Solitary or Dry tree. This vast tree stood alone on a plain with no rivals for ten miles; it was believed that it marked the spot of the battle in which Alexander the Great [of Greece] smashed the last army of Darius [emperor] of Persia [during the fourth century B.C.].[8]

As Marco described it, the tree had green bark on one side and white bark on the other. The wood of the tree was yellow and very tough.[9]

The Assassins

The Polos' route took them south of the Caspian Sea and into the territory of modern Tajikistan. In this area, there once lived a Muslim leader named Hassan-Bin-al-Sabaah, who had formed a group of killers known as the Assassins. The word *assassin* comes from the name of the drug, hashish. Hassan used hashish to drug young men whom he wanted to train as assassins. Then he would take them into a magnificent garden. After the young men awoke, they were surrounded by beautiful young women and enjoyed all the food and drink they desired. Indeed, the young men believed that they had entered paradise.

When Hassan wanted one of the men to assassinate someone, he would give him hashish. The young man would fall asleep and be removed from the garden.

He would then be taken to Hassan and asked to go on a mission. His reward would be to return to the garden.[10] According to Marco Polo, "he would say to the youth: 'Go thou and slay So and So; and when thou returnest my Angels shall bear thee into Paradise. And shouldst thou die, natheless [sic] even so will I send my Angels to carry thee back into Paradise.'"[11] The assassin was sent off to kill. Over several decades, Assassins accounted for the deaths of several prominent leaders in the Middle East.

Known as the Mountain Lord, the leader of the Assassins had built a mountain fortress to protect his garden. He believed that no one could successfully storm its walls. For many years he terrorized the Middle East from his stronghold. But in 1252, the Mongol leader Hülegü led a successful assault against the Assassins' position. The Mongols destroyed the Assassins.

Rare Rubies

The Polos continued westward to the cities of Shibarghan and Balkh. Alexander the Great had visited Balkh during his conquests in the fourth century B.C. Much later, during the thirteenth century, Balkh was captured by the Mongols, who destroyed part of it. From here, the Polos journeyed to the city of Taliqan. This city, like Venice, was rich in salt. The salt was found in mountains south of the city, which drew people from many miles around. They dug the salt with iron picks and used it to preserve their food.

As the Polos traveled through the lands of the Mongols, they reached the province of Badakhshan. As Marco later wrote, this was an area known for its great rubies. The king had them mined from nearby mountains and used the rubies to pay tribute to the Mongol conquerors. Marco wrote of the rubies,

> There is but one special mountain that produces them . . . The stones are dug on the king's account, and no one else dares dig in that mountain on pain of forfeiture of life as well as goods; nor may any one carry the stones out of the kingdom. But the king amasses them all, and sends them to other kings when he had tribute to render, or when he desires to offer a

Source Document

. . . you find an extensive plain, with great abundance of grass and trees, and copious springs of pure water running down through rocks and ravines. In those brooks are found trout and many other fish of dainty kinds; and the air in those regions is so pure, and residence there so healthful, that when the men who dwell below in the towns, and in the valleys and plains, find themselves attacked by any kind of fever or other ailment . . . they lose no time in going to the hills. . . .[12]

The countryside of Badakhshan was beautiful, according to Polo.

friendly present. . . . Thus he acts in order to keep the [rubies] at a high value; for if he were to allow everybody to dig, they would extract so many that the world would be glutted with them, and they would cease to bear any value.[13]

Marco recognized that certain items are valuable only because they are scarce. This is a simple principle of economics that was known to experienced traders like the Polos.

Marco himself had been suffering from a fever for several months. Historians believe that he may have picked it up in Hormuz or perhaps from drinking foul water.[14] But the fever was cured during his stay in Badakhshan.

High Up in the Mountains

During 1273, the Polos' route took them through eastern Afghanistan into western China. Here they reached the plain of Pamir, which lies over fifteen thousand feet, almost three miles, above sea level. It is appropriately known as the roof of the world. Here Marco saw large sheep. He said that the shepherds used the horns from these sheep to make bowls that were used for serving food. Pamir is in the high mountains, where several ranges, including the Hindu Kush Mountain range, come together. Traders regularly journeyed along this route carrying goods back and forth from China to the Middle East and into Europe. Marco commented that fires did not burn as well in Pamir as elsewhere. That is because of the high altitude.

At higher altitudes the air is thinner. This means there is less oxygen, which is necessary to maintain a fire.

The Gobi Desert

The Polos had now traveled over five thousand miles across the Middle East and Asia. But their journey was not yet finished. As they descended from the roof of the world, the Polos entered western China, the province of Kashgar. "The inhabitants live by trade and handicrafts; they have beautiful gardens and vineyards and fine estates, and grow a great deal of cotton," wrote Marco. They also grew hemp, a plant that produces fiber that is used for making rope. Marco commented on the numbers of Nestorian Christians he met here and farther east.[15] He was quite interested in anyone who had religious beliefs that were similar to his own.

This eastern journey took the Polos through four towns as they approached the vast Gobi Desert. The Gobi stretches for five hundred thousand square

The people of Kashgar were very accomplished at farming and making handicrafts.

miles in central Asia. It takes its name from the pebbles, called gobis, that are found at the beginning of the desert. Although the Polos did not need to cross the entire expanse of desert, their route covered part of it. As they reached Lop, on the outskirts of the Gobi, they prepared for their crossing. They loaded up on food and water. They also hired camels, which were used to traveling in the desert. The camels took them across the dry sands.

Hallucinations

Marco Polo wrote extensively about the hallucinations experienced by travelers in the desert. These were often recorded at night, when most people traveled because it was cooler. Polo wrote:

> ". . . [W]hen travelers are on the move by night, and one of them chances to lag behind or to fall asleep or the like, when he tries to gain his company again he will hear spirits talking, and will suppose them to be his comrades. Sometimes the spirits will call him by name; and thus shall a traveler ofttimes be led astray so that he never finds his party. And in this way many have perished."[16]

Oasis

The Polos escaped this fate. They could only move slowly, about fifteen miles a day, because of the intense heat. But no one, apparently, was lost. The Polos carried enough water to supply their needs over the distance between the few oases that exist on the Gobi Desert. An oasis is an area in a desert where water can be found from underground springs. Towns had sprung up at these oases, in part to serve travelers like the Polos. In the past, other traders had covered the long distances across the Gobi. They had also made their way along the route between China and the West.

Out of the Gobi

As they completed their trip across the Gobi, the Polos had covered approximately thirteen hundred miles in China. Beyond the desert, they entered a province where the people mined asbestos. A rich vein of asbestos was discovered in the mountains. "The substance of this vein was then taken and crushed, and when so treated it divides as it were into fibers of wool, which they set forth to dry," wrote Marco. After drying, the fibers were pounded, washed, and spun into wool.[17]

In this area, Marco also commented on the religious beliefs of the people he met. They had a custom of burning their dead, instead of burying them. Marco said, before the body is burned, the townspeople:

> set before it wine and meat . . . All the minstrelsy [musicians] in the town goes playing before the body; and when it reaches the burning place the kinsfolk [family] are prepared with figures cut out of parchment and paper in the shape of men and horses and camels, and also with round pieces of paper like gold coins, and all these they burn along with the corpse. For they say that in the other world the [dead] will be provided with slaves and cattle and money, just

in proportion to the amount of such pieces of paper that has been burnt along with him.[18]

Into China

As Marco Polo drew closer and closer to central China, he began to comment on some of the customs of the people there. He described the yurts used by the Mongols. He explained that most of the domestic chores were done by the Mongol women. The men spent most of their time hunting and training for war. Polo was also fascinated by the religious beliefs of the Mongols. Although they believed in a supreme god, the Mongols spent most of their time worshiping individual household gods. Each home had a statue of a god and his family. The adults prayed to the god regularly for protection for their children, their crops, and their animals. Polo also noted the justice system in the Mongol Empire. Stealing was punished by lashes with a stick. The number of lashes received ranged from seven upward, increased by increments of ten, depending on the seriousness of the crime. The Mongols prized their horses above all other beasts. The punishment for stealing a horse was most severe. Horse theft was punished by execution.

Marco Polo Meets Kublai Khan

In 1274, the Polos journeyed through northern China until they approached one of the palaces of Kublai Khan, located at Chagan-nor. Marco described the vast numbers of birds that the emperor kept at his palace. These included swans, cranes, and falcons. Falconry was a popular sport in China and the West. Falcons were raised in special buildings. They were trained to hunt and kill other birds and small animals. Hunters often took the falcons into wooded areas, keeping them hooded and leashed until the time to hunt. Then the hood was removed and the falcon was let loose to do its hunting.

Kublai Khan had already heard that the Polos were nearing his summer palace at Chengdu. He sent out a special escort to bring them to him. As they entered the palace, they knelt down before the great emperor. He wanted to know all about their journey. The Polos then presented their letter from the pope and the holy oil they had brought from Jerusalem. However, they had to admit that they brought no wise men to describe the principles of Christianity. Then the emperor turned to Marco and asked his father who he was. On finding out, the Khan said: "He is heartily welcome." This was the beginning of Marco Polo's adventures at the court of Kublai Khan.

Chapter 5

Marco Polo and the Great Khan

In "Kubla Khan," published in 1816, the British poet Samuel Taylor Coleridge wrote:

In Xanadu did Kubla Khan
A stately pleasure-dome decree:
Where Alph, the sacred river, ran
Through caverns measureless to man
Down to a sunless sea.
So twice five miles of fertile ground
With walls and towers were girdled round:
And there were gardens bright with sinuous rills [brooks],
Where blossomed many an incense-bearing tree. . . .[1]

Coleridge changed the name of the location of the Khan's summer palace to Xanadu from Chengdu. But it was the same magnificent setting that Marco Polo saw when he arrived there in the thirteenth century. Polo was immediately impressed with the emperor. He described Kublai Khan as a man "of a good stature,

This portrait of Kublai Khan is from a Chinese engraving.

neither tall nor short, but of a middle height. He has a becoming amount of flesh, and is very shapely in all his limbs. His complexion is white and red, the eyes black and fine, and the nose well formed and well set on."[2]

A Palace of Marble

Marco Polo described the splendors of the Khan's palaces. In Chengdu, the emperor had built a huge palace made of the finest marble with rooms of "gilt [gold] and painted with figures of men and beasts and birds, and with a variety of trees and flowers, all executed with such exquisite art that you regard them with delight and astonishment."[3] Inside was a huge hall where six thousand people could gather for a celebration.

Polo was plainly awed by the splendor of Kublai Khan's palace. He explained that the palace was surrounded by a huge sixteen-mile wall. There was also a beautiful park with rivers, brooks, fountains, and meadows. A large lake contained a variety of fish that could be caught for the emperor's dinner table.

A Palace on the Move

In addition to his marble palace, the emperor had also built a portable palace. It was constructed of long bamboo poles. The Great Khan's slaves could easily disassemble this palace and take it with them when the emperor moved. He spent only three months of the year in Chengdu—June, July, and August. Another three months—March, April, and May—were spent on the road in a great hunting expedition.

For this journey, the Great Khan traveled in a large portable pavilion, or tent. It was carried by four elephants. The emperor not only traveled in the pavilion, but he also kept some of his prize falcons inside. If other birds, such as cranes, should be spotted overhead, the emperor would order that the roof of the tent be opened. Then his falcons would be let loose to kill the passing cranes. Hunting with birds was one of the many pleasures that the emperor enjoyed.

The Emperor's Great Hunt

Marco Polo also mentioned that the great emperor liked to hunt deer and bear. For these hunts he had ten thousand men and five thousand hounds to help chase the animals. This was considered an enormous hunting party. It was much larger than any that might be used by a king in western Europe. Polo mentioned all of these numbers to indicate the great wealth and power of Kublai Khan. He also wanted people of the West to be impressed with the great civilization that had been created in China.

The Palace at Beijing

For six months of the year, between September and March, Kublai Khan conducted business from his capital in K'aip'ing. It is located on the site of present-day Beijing, now the capital of China. This palace was surrounded by a series of walls within walls. These were constructed for defense. The outside walls stretched for a mile on each side. At intervals along the walls were eight structures where the emperor kept weapons such as bows and arrows. Each wall also had five gates, which were heavily guarded. Another set of walls was built inside the first set. There were eight small structures and five gates along this second set of walls as well. The emperor's grand palace was enclosed within the second set of walls. "The roof is very lofty," Marco wrote, "and the walls of the Palace are all covered with gold and silver. They are also adorned with representations of dragons, beasts and

Kublai Khan's winter palace at Beijing was vast and surrounded by parks and gardens.

birds, knights and idols. . . . And on the ceiling too you see nothing but gold and silver and painting."[4]

Outside the palace were splendid parks and gardens.

The palace, Marco said, was "so vast, so rich, and so beautiful, that no man on earth could design anything superior to it."[5] In his book *A Description of the World*, published in 1307, Marco sometimes tended to exaggerate the grandeur of the Great Khan's empire. This was because he was very impressed by the emperor and wanted others in the West to be impressed, too.

Marco described the palace's hall, which, he said, could hold thousands of people. It was often filled, especially on feast days. Among the most important feasts were the emperor's birthday on September 28, and the feast of the New Year. In the Mongol calendar, this occurred in February.

Elaborate Feasts

Marco described in elaborate detail the feasts that the great emperor enjoyed. As the festivities began, the Khan would take up a position at one end of the large palace hall. His table was placed on a platform so it would be higher than all the other tables. Here he sat with his sons and nephews and his chief wife. Like any eastern emperor, the Great Khan was permitted more than one wife. In fact, he had four wives and over twenty sons. Below the emperor's table sat his nobles in special places that had been assigned to them. About twenty thousand people could crowd into the hall. Many sat on the floor. Another forty thousand people sat beyond the hall in other dining areas.

The Great Khan and his family drank their wine from large golden containers. The emperor was served his wine and food by some of his nobles. "And when the Emperor is going to drink, all the musical instruments, of which he has vast store of every kind, begin to play." At the same moment, all the nobles bowed before him.[6] At his birthday celebration, the Great Khan was accompanied by twelve thousand nobles. He wore robes made of cloth of gold. His nobles also dressed in rich garments, woven with pearls and other precious jewels.

The Walled City of Taidu

In addition to his palace in the capital, the Great Khan constructed an entirely new city across the river. This was called Taidu. The city was constructed as a square, six miles on each side. There were twelve entrances to the city, with a palace at each entrance. At each gate was a guard of one thousand men. The houses were laid out on square plots, along straight streets. A giant clock in the city struck the hours with a bell. It was extremely rare to have such a clock in the thirteenth century. At night, no one was allowed out on the streets except in an emergency. This kept order in the city.

Feeding Millions

Marco was very impressed by the way Kublai Khan treated his subjects, especially poor farmers. If they suffered a bad harvest, he did not collect any taxes from them. In addition, the government kept supplies of grain in its own storehouses. In fact, there were fifty-eight of these storehouses in the capital, which held several million pounds of grain.[7] If there was a famine in China, the emperor immediately distributed these grain supplies to feed the people. The emperor provided the poor with not only food, but also clothes.

The Mongol Conquest

When Marco Polo arrived in China, the reign of Kublai Khan there was less than two decades old. The Mongols had taken over a civilization that was probably the most advanced in the medieval world. Over the centuries, the Chinese had developed magnificent forms of art, sculpture, and poetry. The Chinese peasants cultivated many acres of well-irrigated land, growing enough rice to feed millions of people. China was knitted together by a large network of canals. These made trade possible throughout the entire country.

The Chinese had developed paper money. Instead of transacting business with heavy bags of gold, merchants used lightweight silk and paper currency. This made trade much easier. The paper money was made from the bark of mulberry trees, which grew extensively in China.

After the conquest, the Mongols integrated China into the rest of their empire. Traders such as the Polos could now move more easily between China, the rest of Asia, and the Middle East. The Mongol government provided relative peace and security for traders making long trips. This meant that Chinese silks and other products could be transported more securely from the East to the West.

In addition to advanced trade and agriculture, the Mongols also inherited a highly developed government. The civil servants in China conducted the government according to the principles of Confucius. The philosopher Confucius (551–479 B.C.) set down ethical standards that were designed to guide the lives of human beings. He believed that by following these standards, men could also create good government.

The Chinese were the first to use paper money. This bank note is from the Ming dynasty, which followed the rule of the Mongols and lasted from 1368 to 1644.

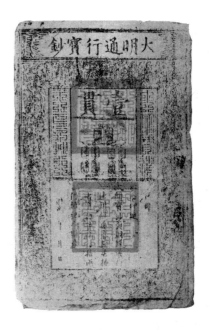

Confucius stressed the importance of education. But along with book learning, he believed, each person must possess the quality of jen. This meant that people must treat others the same way that they would want to be treated. As Confucius said: "Do not impose on others what you yourself do not desire."[8]

Candidates for the civil service were expected to be thoroughly versed in the teachings of Confucius. They also received many years of education and had to pass rigorous examinations for positions in the government. Chinese emperors depended on these civil servants to govern well in the provinces as well as in the central government. During the years following the death of Confucius, China passed through periods of stable government followed by periods of turmoil. The civil servants provided some degree of sound administration and stability amid all the changes. In the years just before the coming of the Mongols, the Chinese bureaucracy increased enormously to deal with an expanding population. The number of civil servants rose from ten thousand to forty thousand.[9] The exams became more rigorous as Chinese emperors wanted to select the best possible people for the government in the capital and the provinces.

Mongol Rule

The Mongols established a new dynasty, called the *Yuan* or *Great Origin*. After consolidating power in the north, Kublai began to attack the Chinese dynasty that controlled southern China. This was the empire of the Song dynasty, a land called Manzi. The Song had once controlled all of China, but they were eventually defeated in the north by the Chin empire, which was in turn defeated by the Mongols.

In the south, the Song continued to rule from their capital at Hangzhou. It was the largest city in the world, with over one million inhabitants. The people of the city lived in houses made of wood and bamboo. A main street, 180 feet wide and called the Imperial Way, ran through the city and ended at the palace of the emperor. The Imperial Way was paved with stone and bricks. Canals also ran through the city, bringing in food and other items. The primary foods were rice and pork.[10]

Before Polo arrived in China, Kublai Khan decided to add southern China to his domain. In 1268, he attacked the large Song city of Xiangyang, which surrendered after a long siege. During the 1270s, the remaining Song strongholds, including Hangzhou, fell. The Mongols were completely victorious by 1279.

With the conquest complete, the Mongols established their control throughout China. Although they built on the existing Chinese government, they also made significant changes. One of these was to divide the people into four social classes. The Mongols at the top of the social-class pyramid. Next were the Western and Central Asians, called the *semu ren*, meaning various foreigners. Below the semu ren were the *Han ren*, who were the people of north China. At the bottom were the *nan ren*, the Chinese of the south. Suddenly, the southern Chinese found themselves at the bottom of society, and many of them were no longer asked to serve in the government.

Instead, the Great Emperor began to depend on Mongols to run the country. He appointed twelve nobles to take charge of the government. These nobles governed the provinces with the help of a staff of judges and clerks. They also appointed the governors of the provinces. In order to tie the huge country together, the Great Khan relied on an efficient messenger service. In fact, he refined the service that had been originally established in other parts of the empire by Genghis Khan. Messengers on the emperor's business would ride between relay stations twenty-five miles from each other. At each station, they would receive a fresh horse. In this way, they could cover up to three hundred miles in a single day.

The most important messages were carried by these horsemen. Less important messages were handled by a series of messengers on foot. They ran between stations set three miles apart. "Each messenger wore a special belt hung with small bells to announce his approach and ensure that his relief was out on the road and ready for a smooth takeover," wrote historian Richard Humble. "This system enabled a message to cover the distance of a normal ten-day journey in twenty-four hours."[11]

With this type of speedy service, the Great Khan communicated quickly with local provinces. He could also receive news of events there. If a revolt broke out, he could immediately dispatch an army to stop it. Since the Mongols were foreigners, they never felt entirely secure on the throne in China. Nor did Kublai Khan trust the Chinese. Therefore, he relied heavily on foreigners for his government. Among them was his chief financial officer, a Muslim named Ahmad. He remained in this position for twenty years. The emperor also welcomed foreigners like the Polos to his court. Indeed, he was apparently very impressed with young Marco. He recognized that Marco was a keen observer of the customs throughout the empire. Marco also revealed that he was more than willing to share what he discovered with the Great Khan.

Marco Polo Works for Kublai Khan

Over the two decades that Marco Polo remained in China, he served as a roving ambassador for Kublai

Khan. He acted as a set of eyes and ears for the emperor. Polo observed what was going on in the realm and reported back to the emperor. On his first trip, Marco Polo set off south and westward from the capital into the interior of China. Along the way, he noted many customs of the people. Some of these customs were completely unfamiliar to him.

Into Sichuan

During one trip, Polo headed southwest to Sichuan province. Among the most important attractions, he described a bridge that spanned a river. The bridge had marble columns on each side that supported a wooden roof that was colorfully painted. Shops were also built along the bridge, creating a covered mall where people came to shop.

Exploring Mien

The men and women of this area also practiced a significant role reversal. After a woman had a baby, she would leave her bed. Her husband would then take over the care of the newborn. He would go to bed for the next forty days. During this time, relatives would visit the baby. Meanwhile, his wife would take care of the household chores.

In his discussion of Mien, Polo described a battle that had been fought before his arrival. This involved a victory by the Mongols over the king of Mien. It led to their control of the country. The king had decided to put a large army into the field to drive out the invading Mongols. Among his soldiers, who numbered sixty thousand, were about two thousand elephants. Troops mounted on these huge beasts were expected to lead the attack against the Mongol cavalry. The Mongol troops were greatly outnumbered and retreated into a forest. There they dismounted. Using trees for protection, they began shooting arrows at the oncoming elephants. The beasts were so frightened when they were hit by the arrows that they ran from the battlefield. Then the Mongol soldiers mounted their horses, charged, and won an overwhelming victory.

Source Document

[They] have their teeth gilt; or rather every man covers his teeth with a sort of golden case made to fit them, both the upper teeth and the under. The men also are wont to gird their arms and legs with bands or [tattoos] pricked in black, and it is done thus; they take five needles joined together, and with these they prick the flesh till the blood comes, and then they rub in a certain black coloring stuff, and this is perfectly indelible. It is considered a piece of elegance and the sign of gentility to have this black band.[12]

On the road to Mien (currently Myanmar, or Burma, in southern Asia), Marco saw people who had tattoos and gold teeth.

Marco Polo was astounded at the beauty of Mien.

Beautiful Pagodas

While he was visiting the capital of Mien, Marco Polo was stunned by the beauty of the pagodas there. Pagodas are temples that look like towers. Two of them stood by the tomb of a king:

> The towers are built of fine stone; and then one of them has been covered with gold a good finger in thickness . . . and the other is covered with silver in like manner so that it seems to be all of solid silver. . . . The upper part of these towers is round, and girt all about with bells, the top of the gold tower with gilded bells and the silver tower with silvered bells, insomuch that whenever the wind blows among these bells they tinkle.[13]

Buddhist pagodas match the grandeur of Catholic cathedrals.

All Around China

Marco Polo also visited Yunan province in China. He described the horses and cattle that were raised by the people who lived there. For money, they relied on shells that were gathered from the ocean. "They have brine wells in this country," he added, "from which they make salt, and all the people of those parts make a living by this salt. The King, too, I can assure you, gets a great revenue from this salt."[14]

On another trip, Polo was sent by the Great Khan to the former Song Empire, known as Manzi. During this visit, Polo visited the former Song capital of Hangzhou. He said that the city had ten major food markets. Markets, he said, were held three days each week, and as many as fifty thousand people shopped at them. The markets offered a wide range of food, including rabbits, pheasants, ducks, and geese.[15]

Polo also described the magnificent lake inside the city:

> . . . all around it are erected beautiful palaces and mansions, of the richest and most exquisite structure

This illustration shows the salt-making process that Marco Polo witnessed in the Yunan province.

that you can imagine, belonging to the nobles of the city. There are also on its shores many abbeys and churches. . . . In the middle of the Lake are two Islands, on each of which stands a rich, beautiful and spacious edifice, furnished in such style as to seem fit for the palace on an Emperor. And when any one of the citizens desired to hold a marriage feast, or to give any other entertainment, it used to be done at one of these palaces.[16]

The Claims of Marco Polo

Marco made a few claims about the role that he, his father, and his uncle played in the defeat of Manzi. First, he claimed that his father and uncle helped the

Great Khan design catapults to capture the city of Xiangyang. Most historians believe that this is very unlikely. "The Mongols already knew how to make [catapults]," Mike Edwards explained, "and the surrender of Xiangyang took place two years before the Polos got to China."[17]

Marco Polo also made another claim. He said that the Great Khan appointed him to serve as governor of Yangzhou, an area in southern China. He said he served for three years. Scholars have debated whether this is possible. Was Marco Polo old enough or experienced enough for such a position? Some scholars believe that Polo was exaggerating. However, others point to the fact that the emperor relied on foreigners in his government. Since he never had enough administrators, it is possible that he did appoint Polo to such a position. Nevertheless, his name does not appear in the history of the area.

At Sea

In addition to his journeys in China, Marco Polo also took sea voyages outside the country. He traveled to Sri Lanka and India. Marco Polo was also familiar with Japan, then called Cipangu. Indeed, the Great Khan tried to conquer it twice, in 1274 and 1281. But each time his ships ran into heavy storms, called typhoons, and were beaten. The Japanese called the second typhoon that destroyed the Khan's fleet *Kamikaze*, meaning "divine wind."

The Polos Request to Leave

By 1285, the Polos had already been in China for more than ten years. Marco and his father and his uncle wanted to return to Venice. However, the Great Khan did not seem interested in letting them go home. Apparently, he had grown attached to the Polos, especially Marco. However, it was clear that the emperor was growing older. He also seemed more and more frail. The Polos feared that if he died, they might not have a secure position under his successors. But there seemed no way for the Polos to convince the Great Khan that it was time for them to go back to Venice.

Then, something happened that changed everything.

Chapter 6

The Polos
Return Home

About 1288, ambassadors arrived at the court of the
Great Khan from his great nephew Arghun, the ruler
of Persia. They explained that his wife, a Mongol
named Bolgana, had recently died. Arghun wanted a
new wife, another Mongol woman, who would be just
like her. A young princess named Kokejin was
selected by Kublai Khan from among the women of
his empire. She was called the Blue Princess, since her
name meant "blue sky."

In 1289, the ambassadors set out for Persia
accompanied by Kokejin. But the journey proved
treacherous because of bandits along the road, so they
returned to Khanbaliq. The Persian ambassadors had
heard about Marco Polo's travels throughout the
empire. They thought that he might be just the man
to lead them back to Persia with the princess.

The Polos were supposed to escort Kokejin to Persia so that she could marry Arghun. Above, a Persian wedding is pictured.

Meanwhile, the Polos had been asking the Great Emperor if they could return to Venice. As a result, Kublai Khan finally agreed that they should go. Before they went, however, he gave them two golden plaques that guaranteed their safe passage through his lands. In addition, he outfitted a force of approximately six hundred men to accompany them on their journey.

The Long Return Journey Begins

In 1291, the Polos left China. Their traveling party included eighteen ships. Each boat had four masts with sails to catch the wind. In addition, they had oarsmen who could row the ships if the wind failed. The Polos and the Blue Princess sailed southward along the coast of China and along Southeast Asia. They were beginning a voyage that would take approximately two years.

After passing through Southeast Asia, a voyage of about three months, the Polos arrived at the island of Sumatra (currently part of Indonesia). As Marco explained, the people there did not grow wheat but produced rice. "They have also great quantities of Indian nuts," he added, "which are good to eat when fresh; being sweet and savory, and white as milk. The inside of the meat of the nut is filled with a liquor like clear fresh water, but better to the taste, and more delicate than wine or any other drink that ever existed."[1]

What Happened at Sumatra?

The travelers were forced to remain in Sumatra for the next five months. Marco Polo says only that it was because of "the weather, which would not [permit] going on."[2] Historians have also speculated that something else may have happened on Sumatra. Polo explained in his book that of the six hundred people who started out on the journey, only eighteen finished the sixty-five-hundred-mile trip to Persia. Many of the travelers may have died in Sumatra because of a disease such as malaria.[3] They may have also been attacked by the people of Sumatra. Polo mentions that the travelers were besieged in camp and forced to defend themselves during their stay on Sumatra. They must have feared attack. Perhaps such an attack occurred, and only a few people survived.[4]

Religions of the East

The Polos eventually left Sumatra along with Kokejin.
They sailed west and briefly landed at other islands.
Throughout his narrative of the years in China and the
trip home, Marco Polo constantly comments on
the religion of the people he met. Some were
Christians; others were Muslims. Many of the people
are what Marco called *Idolaters*. By that term, he
meant followers of religions other than Christianity.
These were often Buddhists. Buddhism is one of the
world's main religions. It was founded in the sixth century B.C. by Siddhartha Gautama. He was called
Buddha, meaning the enlightened one. Buddha taught
that humans can find a path through life that will eliminate desire and suffering. It will lead to Nirvana, the
end of suffering. There were many Buddhists in China
who worshiped in temples or pagodas. Another religion
widely practiced in China was Taoism. Based on the
teachings of Lao Tzu, it originated in the sixth century
B.C. The Taoists followed a philosophy designed to
help them reach self-realization through harmony
with nature.

As Marco Polo reached Sri Lanka and India, he
encountered Hindus. Hinduism is another of the
world's leading religions, founded about 3000 B.C.
Hindus live by the teachings in sacred books called the
Vedas. According to Hinduism, human beings are constantly reincarnated into new lives. In their new lives,
they reap the rewards and punishments of past lives. By
following the teachings of the Vedas, Hindus can

eliminate the suffering of multiple lives and finally unite with God.

In Sri Lanka, Marco commented not only on the religious beliefs he encountered, but on other experiences as well. Sometimes he exaggerated the wonders that he saw. Perhaps he wanted to impress the readers of his book. He also may have believed that a little exaggeration would grab their attention. In his description of Sri Lanka, for example, he said that the king owned sapphires, topazes, and amethysts. But his prize possession was a ruby, according to Marco, "which is the finest and biggest in the world. . . . It is about a palm in length, and as thick as a man's arm; to look at, it is the most resplendent object upon earth; it is quite free from flaw and as red as fire."[5]

Exploring India

From Sri Lanka, the travelers journeyed to India. They traveled along the Malabar Coast, the west coast of India. Here Marco Polo witnessed the practice of pearl diving. It continues in various parts of the world today. "When the men have got into the small boats they jump into the water and dive to the bottom," he wrote,

> And there they find the shells that contain the pearls and these they put into a net bag tied around the waist, and mount up to the surface with them, and then dive anew. When they can't hold their breath any longer they come up again, and after a little down they go once more, and so they go on all day.[6]

Polo was a keen observer of local customs, especially when they differed from those in western Europe. In one area he noted that people were completely naked except for a small cloth tied around their middles. Even the king, he said, wore almost nothing except a magnificent necklace. It was made of jewels, including rubies, sapphires, emeralds, and pearls. The Malabar Coast was a popular trading area. Merchants from as far away as Hormuz in Persia brought horses to the area. And ships also came there from southern China to trade.

Burning Rituals

Marco Polo may have been among the first Europeans to describe the ancient ritual of *suttee* that was practiced in India. According to this custom, a wife would place herself on the funeral pyre, or pile of wood, of her dead husband. Here she would burn along with his dead body and atone for her sins. Widows had no position of importance in India; therefore, death seemed to be an acceptable alternative. The practice had been followed for centuries in India and other cultures.[7]

A similar practice occurred when the local king died. His nobles rode with his dead body to the fire where it was to be burned. As the fire consumed his body, they "cast themselves into the fire round about his body, and suffer themselves to be burnt along with him," Polo explained. "For they say they have been his comrades in this world, and that they ought also to keep him company in the other world."[8]

In thirteenth-century India, many spectators came out to watch a widow jump or be thrown onto her husband's funeral pyre.

Bathing and Sleeping in India

Marco Polo also commented on the practice of bathing in India. Some Indian people bathed twice a day. In the West, baths were avoided for fear they might lead to illness. Another practice that Polo found quite interesting was the sleeping arrangement of some of the Indians. They made beds of light bamboo sticks and pulled them up to the ceiling at night for sleeping. This enabled them to avoid the tarantulas that crawled along the floor. Tarantulas are large spiders with fierce bites.

Mining for Diamonds With Eagles

As he sailed along the coast of India and anchored at its ports, Marco Polo described an area where huge diamonds were found in the rivers. Diamonds also lay at the bottom of deep ravines. Indeed, the ravines were so deep that men could not climb into them. In order to obtain the diamonds, the Indians of the area used a unique approach. Marco said,

> They take with them pieces of flesh, as lean as they can get, and these they cast into the bottom of a valley. Now there are numbers of white eagles that haunt those mountains and feed upon the serpents. When the eagles see the meat thrown down they pounce upon it and carry it up to some rocky hill top where they begin to rend [tear] it. But there are men on the watch, and as soon as they see that the eagles have settled they raise a loud shouting to drive them away. And when the eagles are thus frightened away the men recover the pieces of meat, and find them full of diamond which have stuck to the meat down in the bottom.[9]

Indigo

In his trip through India, Marco observed the process of producing indigo, a blue dye. The source of indigo was an herb. The indigo plants were harvested, then placed in large vats of water that were set in the sun to boil. Eventually, the indigo sunk to the bottom of the vats. When the water was stirred, the blue indigo dye was produced. The processed indigo was shipped to many parts of the world, where it was used to dye clothing.

As Marco journeyed westward he came to the city of Kollam. This was also an area where indigo was grown. Kollam, located on the coast, was a thriving trading city. Merchants from China and the Arabian

Peninsula regularly sailed here to trade. Marco mentioned that he saw black lions, beautiful parrots, and peacocks in Kollam, unlike any animals he had seen in the West.

Escaping Pirates

As they sailed along the coast, Marco and his companions were constantly on the lookout for pirates. "Their method," he wrote, "is to join in fleets of 20 or 30 of these pirate vessels together, and then they form what they call a sea cordon, that is, they drop off till there is an interval of 5 or 6 miles between ship and ship, so that they cover something like an hundred miles of sea." He said some of the pirates,

> force merchants to swallow a stuff called *Tamarindi* mixed in sea-water, which produces violent purging. This is done in case the merchants, on seeing their danger, should have swallowed their most valuable stones and pearls. And in this way the pirates secure the whole.[10]

Fortunately, the Polos seemed to have escaped the pirates. Marco does not explain how they managed to do so.

To Persia

From India, they headed westward to the Persian Gulf. Along the way, they encountered two islands that Marco called "Male" and "Female." Historians do not know which islands these were. According to Marco, only men lived on the "male" island, while the other island was inhabited only by women. The men visited their wives, who lived on the female island, for three months each year—March, April, and May. Then the men returned to their island. If children were born, the girls lived with their mothers. The boys also stayed with their mothers, but only until they were fourteen. Then they went to live with their fathers.

The Death of Arghun

Marco and his fellow travelers reached Hormuz about 1293 or 1294. This was the same place the Polos had visited more than twenty years earlier. When the Polos arrived at the court of Arghun, they discovered that he had died. Arghun had been a great warrior, according to Marco. He had helped defend the Persian Empire against attack. Then he had been forced to defend his throne against an uncle who wanted it for himself.

Arghun of Persia died in 1292, a year or two before Marco Polo reached Hormuz. Above, a typical Persian funeral is pictured.

Arghun's uncle was eventually killed, and Arghun consolidated his power in 1286. He ruled for only six years, until his death. His brother Kaikhatu had taken his throne and driven out Arghun's son, Prince Ghazan. Apparently Kaikhatu did not want his brother's intended wife, no matter how beautiful she was. Instead, he ordered the Polos to take her to Prince Ghazan. He was defending the northern frontier of Persia.

Back to Venice

Eventually, the Polos found Prince Ghazan and his army. They delivered the princess to him. It was difficult for the Polos to leave her, because they had all developed a deep liking for each other.[11]

The Polos then retraced their steps and returned to the court of Kaikhatu. From there, the travelers headed north to the Black Sea. Arriving at Trebizond, the Polos found that much had changed since they last visited there. A descendant of the Byzantine emperor had taken the throne. He forced out the Christian rulers who had captured the city in 1204. The Byzantine emperor had been assisted by the Genoese Navy, which was becoming more powerful. As a reward for their help, he gave them special trading rights in the Byzantine Empire. They received all the benefits that the Venetians had enjoyed in the past. The Venetian traders had lost their position in the empire.

As a result, the Polos encountered hostility when they reached Trebizond. In fact, they were forced to give up part of the treasure they had amassed in China. This was a form of tax that the Byzantine emperor required them to pay before they could leave the city. From Trebizond, the Polos traveled south to Constantinople, which they had last seen in 1271. From there, they returned to Venice, arriving home in 1295. By this time, Marco had reached the age of forty-one. His father and uncle were old men. Marco had been gone for twenty-four years.

Although Marco may have thought that his adventures were finally at an end, there was still at least one more awaiting him. This would lead to the writing of a book that would become one of the classics of Europe.

Chapter 7

The Legacy of Marco Polo

Once Marco Polo returned to Venice, he found that his city was at war with Genoa. The two Italian cities were contending for control of rich trading routes in the Mediterranean Sea and around Constantinople.

In 1298, Marco sailed aboard a galley that was part of the Venetian war fleet. Some experts believe that he may have even commanded the galley.

On September 7, a naval battle took place between the Venetians and the Genoese near Korcula, or Curzola. It is an island near the Dalmatian coast. The Venetian fleet was destroyed. An estimated sixty-six galleys were captured. Seven thousand sailors were killed and another seventy-four hundred were captured. One of these was Marco Polo. According to one historian: "He was captured because he threw himself and his galley to the front of the battle and because he

Marco Polo's galley heads into battle near Korcula.

was fighting for his country with great courage and then injured, in chains, he was taken off to Genoa."[1]

Jailed!

After he was thrown in jail, Polo met another sailor. His name was Rustichello. He had been captured during the 1280s in a naval battle between Pisa and Genoa. The Genoese had defeated the Pisans, who were also fighting for control of trade routes. Rustichello was a part-time author, who had written a book about King Arthur. King Arthur was a legendary king of England during the sixth century A.D. Marco Polo and Rustichello struck up a friendship in prison. Since Rustichello already had experience as a published author, they decided to work together on a book.

Marco Polo had probably always planned to write a book about his adventures in China. Historians believe that he took notes during his travels there. They do not think that Polo could have remembered all of his adventures. He needed to write them down. The fact that he kept notes probably indicates that he planned to eventually write a book.[2]

Marco Polo's Book Takes Shape

Polo probably sent to Venice for his notes. His father may have then had them shipped to his prison cell in Genoa. Based on these notes, his book began to take shape. Since Marco Polo was not trained as a writer, he relied heavily on the skills of Rustichello. The Pisan gave Polo's plain words a flourish that would appeal to readers in medieval Europe. For example, the book began with the words: "Great Princes, Emperors, and Kings, Dukes and Marquises, Counts, Knights, and Burgesses! And People of all degrees who desire to get knowledge of the various races of mankind and of the diversities of the sundry [various] regions of the World, take this Book and cause it to be read to you."[3] These were similar to the grand-sounding words that Rustichello had used to open his book about the legends of King Arthur and his court.

Polo's book, *A Description of The World*, covers the first journey to China by his father and uncle during the 1260s. It also includes Polo's travels across Asia to China during the 1270s, a description of the grandeur of Kublai Khan's court, Polo's trip to Myanmar, his journey through South China, as well as his adventures in Sri Lanka, Sumatra, and India.

The book was in part a travelogue, or a piece of writing about travel. Marco Polo wanted to tell people who had never been to the East what they could expect to find there. Polo had a sharp eye for all the products that were made for sale to traders. After all, he was a Polo, a member of a Venetian trading family. He also talked about the marvels that he saw during his travels. The people of the thirteenth century, in which Polo lived, believed in many wonders that could not be explained. This period came before the age of scientific discovery, which would not begin until several centuries later. Therefore, people were very impressed by unexplained marvels.

For example, Polo talked about the oil that sprung from the ground near the Caspian Sea. This seemed like a miracle that had no explanation. He also related some of the legends that were part of the medieval world. For instance, he discussed the tombs of the three wise men, who had visited the Christ child in Bethlehem. These men were supposedly buried in Saveh, although there was no evidence to support this.

In addition to these stories, Polo also related customs that were bound to interest his readers in the West. For example, he discussed some peoples he met who went entirely naked. And he talked about the many wives and children of the Great Khan. All of these customs would have seemed very strange and forbidden—yet intriguing—to readers in the West.

Fact Vs. Fiction

Ever since his book was published, experts have wondered whether Marco Polo actually experienced all the adventures that he claimed to have had. If he went to China, they wondered, why did he not talk about the Great Wall? This was an enormous defensive structure that had been built during the third century B.C. Also, why did he not mention the elaborate Chinese ceremony for drinking tea?

Historian John Larner points out that much of the Great Wall "had fallen down by the thirteenth century. Almost everything the tourist is normally shown today," he adds, "was built in the sixteenth century. . . . Tea-culture at that time had not reached North and Central China, where Polo mostly resided."[4] In other words, Polo could not be expected to comment on things that he did not see.

Some experts believed that Marco Polo and his father and uncle never went to China, but journeyed only as far as the Middle East. Here they heard stories about the empire of Kublai Khan. Larner, however, strongly disagrees. As he put it:

> if they were in fact spending their time carrying on trade in any of the western Mongol [lands] . . . there were, already by the 1280s, plenty of Italian merchants who would have resided there with them, and who could have denounced their claim to have been elsewhere.[5]

Also, the Polos could not have received the gold plaques they carried back to Venice from anyone other than the Great Khan. In addition, Marco Polo's knowledge of southern China was too detailed to have been gathered in any other way than by visiting the area. He was also the first European to talk about Cipangu, now called Japan.

Publishing the Book

The book was published in 1307. The printing press was invented in Europe during the 1400s by the German Johannes Gutenberg. About the same time, William Caxton printed the first book in England. The book was among the first to be printed during the late fifteenth century.

From the time of its original appearance, Marco Polo's book was a bestseller in Europe. Yet, there were always people who doubted some of what Polo wrote. There is no question that he sometimes exaggerated what he saw.[6] But most of his account was probably accurate. The fact was that many Europeans had trouble believing that such an advanced civilization could exist in the East.

Polo did not grow wealthy from the sales of his book. Publishing in the Middle Ages was nothing like it is today. Only a small number of copies were laboriously hand-copied. However, the book appeared in more translations than any other manuscript of the period.

Although Polo had begun his book in a Genoese prison, he was released in 1299 along with Rustichello. The two men then completed the manuscript. Meanwhile, Polo lived in Venice, where he eventually married and had three daughters. Just before his death in 1324, he was still being questioned about the authenticity of what he had written. "I did not write half of what I saw," he said.[7]

Polo had been very impressed with the culture in China. This was because it seemed far more advanced than the culture of Europe. Cities, such as Hangzhou, were much larger than any European city. The Chinese also seemed more technologically advanced,

In the prison in Genoa, Marco Polo (left) and Rustichello work on A Description of the World.

having first invented the mechanical clock and paper money. Polo wanted to make sure that Europeans were aware of this great culture.

Influence of Marco Polo's Book

After his death, Marco Polo's book began to influence maps of the world. Fourteenth-century maps, for example, show China as it was described by Marco Polo. Early encyclopedias developed during the fifteenth century credit Marco Polo for his accurate observations of the Far East. Other travelers who journeyed east during the same period confirmed what Polo had described in his book. During the same century, some maps also reflected the writings of Marco Polo and his descriptions of China and Japan.

Historians have debated the influence of Marco Polo's writings on the voyages of Christopher Columbus. The Italian explorer made his first trip to the New World in 1492. However, Columbus was not looking for the Western Hemisphere. Instead, he was hoping to find a shorter trade route to China and Japan by sailing west. Some experts believe that Columbus had read Marco Polo's book before setting off on his first voyage. Polo's description of China and Japan, these experts believed, influenced Columbus's decision to embark on his search for a new route to the Far East. However, historian John Larner believes that Columbus first read Polo's book after his first voyage in 1492. He cites a letter received by Columbus from a friend late in 1497 or early in 1498. It said that he would send him a copy of the book.[8]

Regardless of when Columbus actually read Marco Polo's book, there is no doubt that he was influenced by him. The maps of the period that Columbus used showed the impact of Polo's book. After the fifteenth century, *A Description of The World* went through more printings. The book became especially popular during the eighteenth and nineteenth centuries. In this period Europeans were making more and more voyages to China for trade. During the nineteenth century, Japan was also visited by western traders. In 1853, U.S. ships under the command of Commodore Matthew Perry steamed into Japan. At this time, the Japanese islands began to trade with the West.

As the East and the West grew closer together, more and more readers became interested in the travels of Marco Polo. They seemed to recognize his accomplishments. As one historian put it: "He was the first Traveller to trace a route across the whole longitude of Asia, naming and describing kingdom after kingdom which he had seen with his own eyes. . . . The first Traveller to reveal China in all its wealth and vastness. . . ." as well as many other countries, including Sumatra, India, Java, and Sri Lanka.[9] Marco Polo's travels were an unparalleled achievement.

Timeline

1095—Pope Urban II calls first crusade.

1167—Birth of Genghis Khan, Mongol leader.

1204—Venetians and European allies sack Constantinople.

1210—Genghis Khan invades China.

1215—Birth of Kublai Khan.

1220—Mongols conquer Persian Empire.

1227—Death of Genghis Khan.

1234—Mongols take control of northern China.

1241—Victory of Mongols over European knights in Poland; Mongols threaten western Europe.

1253—Niccolo and Maffeo Polo set sail from Venice to Constantinople.

1254—Birth of Marco Polo.

1258—Mongols capture Baghdad.

1260—Kublai Khan becomes emperor of Mongols.

1261—Niccolo and Maffeo Polo enter Bolgara in Mongol Empire.

1265—Polos travel to China.

1266—Polos meet Kublai Khan and return to the West.

1269—Polos arrive home in Venice.

1271—Marco Polo leaves Venice for China, accompanied by his father and his uncle.

1274—Polos reach China.

1274—Marco Polo lives in China.
–1291

1291—Polos travel from China to Venice.
–1295

1298—Marco Polo captured by Genoese in naval battle and imprisoned.

1299—Marco Polo begins writing book.

1307—Marco Polo publishes his book.

1324—Marco Polo dies in Venice.

Chapter Notes

Chapter 1. Riches of the East

1. Richard Humble, *Marco Polo* (New York: G.P. Putnam's Sons, 1975), pp. 194–195.

2. Maurice Collis, *Marco Polo* (New York: New Directions, 1960), p. 179.

3. Henry Hart, *Venetian Adventurer: The Life and Times of Marco Polo* (Stanford, Calif.: Stanford University Press, 1947), p. 175.

Chapter 2. Citizens of Venice

1. Thomas Caldecot Chubb, *The Venetians: Merchant Princes* (New York: Viking, 1968), p. 52.

2. Henry H. Hart, *Venetian Adventurer: The Life and Times of Marco Polo* (Stanford, Calif.: Stanford University Press, 1947), pp. 4–5.

3. Chubb, p. 85.

4. Ibid., pp. 15–16.

5. John Julius Norwich, *A History of Venice* (New York: Knopf, 1982), p. 73.

6. Hart, p. 10.

7. Norwich, p. 134.

Chapter 3. The Polos and the Mongol Empire

1. Henry Hart, *Venetian Adventurer: The Life and Times of Marco Polo* (Stanford, Calif.: Stanford University Press, 1947), p. 14.

2. Mary Hull, *The Travels of Marco Polo* (San Diego, Calif.: Lucent Books, 1995), p. 22.

3. Robert Marshall, *Storm from The East: From Genghis Khan to Khubilai Khan* (Berkeley, Calif.: University of California Press, 1993), p. 40.

4. Ibid., p. 49.

5. Hart, p. 22.

6. Morris Rossabi, *Khubilai Khan: His Life and Times* (Berkeley, Calif.: University of California Press, 1988), pp. 148–149.

Chapter 4. Marco Polo Travels to China

1. Mike Edwards, "The Adventures of Marco Polo, Part I," *National Geographic*, May 2001, p. 3.

2. Henry Yule, ed., *The Book of Ser Marco Polo* (New York: Charles Scribner's Sons, 1929), vol. 1, p. 46.

3. Edwards, p. 4.

4. Yule, p. 78.

5. Edwards, p. 6.

6. Yule, p. 90.

7. Yule, p. 108.

8. Richard Humble, *Marco Polo* (New York: G.P. Putnam's Sons, 1975), p. 73.

9. Yule, pp. 127–128.

10. Sherif Nour, "For Two Centuries, The Original Assassins Held The Middle East in a Perpetual Grip of Terror," *Military History*, October 2002.

11. Yule, p. 143.

12. Ibid., pp. 158–159.

13. Ibid., p. 157.

14. Humble, p. 80.

15. Yule, pp. 181–182.

16. Ibid., p. 197.

17. Ibid., p. 213.

18. Ibid., p. 204.

Chapter 5. Marco Polo and the Great Khan

1. William Keach, ed., *Samuel Taylor Coleridge: The Complete Poems* (London: Penguin, 1997), pp. 250–251.

2. Henry Yule, ed., *The Book of Ser Marco Polo* (New York: Charles Scribner's Sons, 1929), vol. 1, p. 356.

3. Ibid., p. 298.

4. Ibid., pp. 363–364.

5. Ibid., p. 364.

6. Ibid., p. 383.

7. Morris Rossabi, *Khubilai Khan: His Life and Times* (Berkeley, Calif.: University of California Press, 1988), p. 120.

8. J.A.G. Roberts, *A Concise History of China* (Cambridge, Mass.: Harvard University Press, 1999), p. 15.

9. Ibid., p. 86.

10. Jacques Gernet, *Daily Life in China on The Eve of the Mongol Invasion, 1250–1276* (New York: Macmillan, 1962), pp. 27, 41, 45, 114.

11. Richard Humble, *Marco Polo* (New York: G.P. Putnam's Sons, 1975), p. 133.

12. Henry Yule, ed., *The Book of Ser Marco Polo* (New York: Charles Scribner's Sons, 1929), vol. 2, pp. 84–85.

13. Ibid., p. 110.

14. Ibid., p. 66.

15. Ibid., p. 201.

16. Ibid., pp. 186–187.

17. Mike Edwards, "Marco Polo in China, Part II," *National Geographic*, June 2001, p. 7.

Chapter 6. The Polos Return Home

1. Henry Yule, *The Book of Ser Marco Polo* (New York: Charles Scribner's Sons, 1929), vol. 2, p. 293.

2. Ibid., p. 292.

3. Mike Edwards, "Marco Polo, Part III: Journey Home," *National Geographic*, July 2001, pp. 4–5.

4. Richard Humble, *Marco Polo* (New York: G.P. Putnam's Sons, 1975), p. 191.

5. Yule, p. 313.

6. Ibid., p. 332.

7. *The Columbia Encyclopedia, Fifth Edition* (New York: Columbia University Press, 1993), p. 2662.

8. Yule, p. 339.

9. Ibid., pp. 360–361.

10. Ibid., pp. 389, 392.

11. Humble, p. 199.

Chapter 7. The Legacy of Marco Polo

1. Dr. Zivan Filippi, "The Battle Before Korcula," *Korcula.net*, n.d., <http://www.korcula.net/mpolo/mpolo7. htm> (January 29, 2003).

2. Richard Humble, *Marco Polo* (New York: G.P. Putnam's Sons, 1975), p. 213.

3. Henry Yule, ed., *The Book of Ser Marco Polo* (New York: Charles Scribner's Sons, 1929), vol. 1, p. 1.

4. John Larner, *Marco Polo and The Discovery of The World* (New Haven: Yale University Press, 1999), p. 59.

5. Ibid., p. 61.

6. Humble, p. 213.

7. Mike Edwards, "Marco Polo, Part III: Journey Home," *National Geographic*, July 2001, p. 10.

8. Larner, p. 155.

9. Yule, pp. 106–107.

Further Reading and Internet Addresses

Books

Hull, Mary. *The Travels of Marco Polo*. San Diego, Calif.: Lucent Books, 1995.

Macdonald, Fiona. *Marco Polo: A Journey Through China*. Danbury, Conn.: Franklin Watts, 1998.

———. *The World in the Time of Marco Polo*. Philadelphia: Chelsea House, 2001.

Stefoff, Rebecca. *Marco Polo and the Medieval Explorers*. Philadelphia: Chelsea House, 1992.

Internet Addresses

"Marco Polo and Korcula, the birthplace of Marco Polo." *Korcula.net*. n.d. <http://www.korcula.net/mpolo/>.

"Marco Polo and his Travels." *Silkroad Foundation*. 1997–2000. <http://www.silk-road.com/toc/index.html>.

Internet Medieval Sourcebook. January 8, 2000. <http://www.fordham.edu/halsall/sbook.html>.

Index